Vegan

CUPCAKES

Delicious and Dairy-Free Recipes to Sweeten the Table

VEGAN CUPCAKES

Delicious and Dairy-Free Recipes to Sweeten the Table

Toni Rodríguez

Translated by Gladis Castillo

Skyhorse Publishing

Thanks to . . .

The Oceano Ambar team for having done an incredible job and giving me the opportunity to publish my second book. Becky Lawton and her team, for making these cupcakes look like the most beautiful things in the world. My Lujuria Vegana team for sweetening the world in the most ethical way possible. My professional friends, who always teach me something new: Petit chef, Eugeni Muñoz, Sergi Vela, Adriana Ortemberg, Javier Medvedovsky, Restaurante VegWorld, Chiara, Adri and Eva of Gopal, Tano, Lola, Andrea, Gervás of Boom Boom Rest, Dani of Restaurante Vegania . . . And many friends who are not in this profession but who made it possible for this dream to come true.

Thanks also to Animanaturalis, Igualdad Animal, PETA, and many other organizations that are fighting for a better world for animals. Finally, all this would not be possible without the support of Bere, my partner, as well as my family members, who are always by my side for better or for worse. I am eternally grateful.

Original title: CUPCAKES VEGANOS
© 2013 Toni Rodríguez
© Becky Lawton, for the photography
© 2013 Editorial Océano, S.L.
(Barcelona, Spain)

English translation © 2015 by Skyhorse Publishing

Skyhorse Publishing books may be purchased in bulk at special discounts for sales promotion, corporate gifts, fund-raising, or educational purposes. Special editions can also be created to specifications. For details, contact the Special Sales Department, Skyhorse Publishing, 307 West 36th Street, 11th Floor, New York, NY 10018 or info@skyhorsepublishing.com.

Skyhorse® and Skyhorse Publishing® are registered trademarks of Skyhorse Publishing, Inc.®, a Delaware corporation.

Visit our website at www.skyhorsepublishing.com.

10 9 8 7 6 5 4 3 2 1

Library of Congress Cataloging-in-Publication Data is available on file.

Cover design by Laura Klynstra
Cover photo courtesy of Oceano Ambar

ISBN: 978-1-63450-345-7
Ebook ISBN: 978-1-63450-903-9

Printed in China

Contents

So it began

Only about ten years have gone by. It was in 2005 when I made my first cake, a carrot cake with vegan icing. I did it without measuring the ingredients, and it came out very rich and fluffy. That encouraged me to continue and, without a recipe, I made a second cake. That second time, fortune did not smile down on me and the result was terrible. So I stopped improvising and started to learn how to successfully prepare vegan cake recipes that I came across on the Internet. There were very few so I needed more material to keep learning. That is when my friend Pantxo brought me a vegan bakery book from the US. My English was minimal and words like "frosting," "topping," "whipped," or "dough" sounded Chinese to me. The book did not include photographs and with such few references, the process was complicated. So I made just one cake. I was not ready to give up and bought a few pastry books but none of them were vegan. I followed the measurements and procedures in each recipe but I simply substituted ingredients such as eggs and milk.

While practicing at home with all kinds of cakes, fillings, creams . . . I kept looking into new possibilities and using different ingredients. In a specialized shop I found a product called "egg replacer," which is an egg substitute that is made with potato starch, tapioca starch, and xanthan gum. I just had to give it a try since several recipes were included in the box. I chose to start with muffins, to see how it went . . . I bought cupcake liners and followed all the steps in the recipe. But without a cupcake pan, the liners fell apart and the dough mixed together. Undeterred, I heated the oven to 338° F (170° C) and after a little while I was holding my first muffin. Once I tasted it, I immediately noticed that its texture was different from everything that I had prepared up until that point.

Encouraged by the result, I decorated the muffins with chocolate cream using a pastry bag. They were really delicious and we immediately devoured them.

Such were my first steps into vegan baking. Since then I have made thousands of cupcakes of all kinds: dark chocolate, white chocolate with no milk, carrot, red velvet, dried fruit, caramel, apricot, mango, coconut, raspberry, strawberry, pumpkin, zucchini, pistachio, hazelnut, coffee, blueberries . . . And always with different creams made with vegan cheese, lemon, orange, dark and white chocolates, toffee, peanut, hazelnut, liqueur . . . A long and ever-increasing list of ingredients, flavors, and sensations.

From New York to the world

The origin of American cupcakes dates back to the early nineteenth century, but it was not until 2008 when Magnolia Bakery at 401 Bleecker St. in *Sex and the City* made them famous worldwide. Soon after, these delicious cupcakes timidly invaded Europe, where they began to be seen in bakeries, cafés, restaurants, and tearooms: sweet, savory, in colorful liners, without liners, as big as petit fours, gigantic versions, with different colors and flavors . . . Gradually, this trend started to spread and shops began to sell the required ingredients, utensils, and recipes to prepare them at home.

And from the world to our home

Cupcakes are a sweet treat made from wheat flour, sugar, eggs, butter, milk, baking powder, and vanilla that I now make available to those who are lactose intolerant, those allergic to dairy and eggs, or those who simply prefer not to use animal-based ingredients for ethical and ideological reasons.

In this book you will find a number of recipes made with different creams, fillings, cakes, cookies, icing, or glazes—cupcakes for every taste and experience level that I have personally selected from my favorite recipes. My main objective is for the reader to become familiar with different methods for creating cakes, creams, and toppings. Once you master the technique, measuring, and proper ingredient use, the rest is a matter of imagination, daring, and curiosity, three basic "ingredients" that are fundamental for creating healthy and deliciously perfect vegan cupcakes.

Vegan bakery

The history of vegan pastry is relatively recent. There is very little written about it, but its main development and evolution could be in the United States, where most bakeries specializing in cakes made with 100 percent vegetarian ingredients without eggs, milk, or honey are based.

That is because Americans love their sweets. From coast to coast, there are tempting arrays of strudels, cannoli, donuts, palmiers, muffins, cupcakes, cheesecakes, cinnamon rolls, plum cakes, galettes, macaroons, ice creams, sorbets, cookies, profiteroles, puddings, croissants, crumbles, tarts, pralines, bonbons, biscotti, carrot cakes, verrines, wafers, shortbreads, nougatines . . . An endless menu of possibilities prepared according to the customs and ethnic roots of each area as well as the multiculturalism that characterizes this vast country. Moreover, Americans have a long history of working to defend animal rights, a long tradition of organizations heavily involved in defending animal rights that hold numerous events, marches, campaigns against animal cruelty, etc.

To all this, one must add the long baking tradition and excellent customer service provided in this vast country. This has allowed American vegans to enjoy a wide range of products made without animal ingredients, and not just in specialty shops but in most shops, restaurants, and cafés.

Lujuria Vegana, a sweet and healthy temptation
The European continent has managed to develop special variations of vegan pastry tradition that originated in the United States. Until recently, it was virtually unknown in Europe. Fortunately, that trend has changed and now in cities like London, Paris, Madrid, or Barcelona there are businesses that specialize in selling and providing vegan products.

True, there are still too few vegan bakeries, but many entrepreneurs have begun to bake delicious and beautiful vegan sweets that they sell to a growing number of restaurants and cafés so people can more easily access them. Such is the case with Lujuria Vegana (www.lujuriavegana.com), my personal and professional adventure that is the inspiration for this book. Since early 2011, this young company has prepared and served all types of cakes, cupcakes, galettes, and pastries that are free of any animal ingredients to a faithful and ever-increasing large clientele. Our products sold abroad have earned the admiration of both vegan and non-vegan customers alike. Our bright glazes, fluffy mousses, creamy fillings, tender cakes, and elaborate decorations are up to par with those of American vegan bakeries.

An upward trend

Gradually, Spain is becoming a good model for the preparation of vegan pastry, not just in Europe, but globally. In recent times, the demand for this type of dessert has grown considerably. More and more people are willing to enjoy a good vegan cake after lunch or dinner, an assortment of cupcakes as snacks, or a treat between meals. It is becoming a trend that traditional bakeries, by offering croissants and palmiers without dairy or eggs; brownies or carrot cake without eggs; and donuts, cupcakes, marzipan, cookies, etc., are catching onto. Now it is easier to go out to eat or drink and have a completely vegan sweet alternative.

I hope you enjoy this book's explanations and vegan recipes. In it you will find many recipes that I use to make all types of cakes, pies, cookies, brownies . . . which can help you get more out of the exciting and gratifying world of vegan pastries. Bon appétit!

Main ingredients

Before making any vegan cupcake recipes in this book, take a moment to familiarize yourself with the most commonly used ingredients. In a good vegan baker's kitchen there should always be:

Starch. Also known as amylum, it is a carbohydrate present in almost all vegetables. It is used to thicken creams, cakes, mousses, etc.

Sugar and syrups. White sugar, brown sugar, maple syrup, molasses, agave syrup, stevia . . . use any of these sweeteners in vegan desserts.

White chocolate with no milk (vegan). Made from cacao butter, sugar, vanilla, soy lecithin, and, in some cases, rice flour to give it more body. There are few brands that manufacture it so it can be difficult to find.

Dark chocolate. Made with cacao paste and butter, soy lecithin, and sugar. Some are flavored, especially with vanilla. It contains no milk and its cacao percentage varies between 50 and 99 percent.

Vegan cream cheese. Cream made with tofu, water, vegetable protein, and non-hydrogenated vegetable fats. It is used to make cheesecakes, creams, mousses, and fillings.

Spices. Vegetable flavoring used both in cooking and baking to flavor all kinds of treats. Some of the most common spices for sweet recipes are vanilla, nutmeg, cinnamon, cumin, and coriander.

Leavening agent. It is used to give biscuits their light and spongy texture. It is also known as baking soda and as baking powder, and its basic ingredient is sodium bicarbonate.

Liqueur. Alcoholic drink flavored with fruit, herbs, or spices. It is often used as a topping for cakes, creams, mousses, and fillings. You may also use non-alcoholic liqueurs.

Margarine. Created in 1860 as a substitute for butter so that the lower classes of the time could have access to this food, it is a water-based emulsion mixed with vegetable fats. Bakeries often use dense margarines with 80 percent fat, while households use softer margarine that typically does not exceed 55 percent fat. As a healthier option, avoid those that contain trans fats.

Vegetable cream. Product made from soy milk, oat milk, or almond milk. It is an essential ingredient in all kinds of creams or mousses, although it is also often used to make cakes.

Nut paste. Liquid, raw, or roasted paste that is usually made from a single nut (almond, pistachio, macadamia, hazelnut, pine nut, cashew, walnut . . .) and may include some sunflower oil, depending on the nut's density.

Praline. Sugar mixed with one or more nuts. Used for making chocolates, creams, and fillings. The sugar is usually caramelized to provide a particularly special taste.

Fruit puree. Crushed and strained fruit that may include a certain percentage of sugar. It is very easy to use due to not having to wash, peel, remove the seed, and shred every piece of natural fruit.

Tofu. Vegetable cheese made with soy milk that is used to enhance creams or biscuits.

Vanilla. Pod-shaped fruit that comes from a wild orchid's vine (*Vanilla planifolia*), originally from Mexico. It is an excellent and sought-after flavoring in baking.

What do you need?

To make vegan cupcakes you will need a series of tools that will make your work much easier and more comfortable. The basic elements to consider and that your kitchen cannot do without are as follows:

Scale. No other element is more valuable for baking. It allows you to accurately weigh all the ingredients needed to make cupcakes, without worrying about making mistakes, and ensuring the outcome.

Electric mixer. Essential for beating dough and to whip cream quickly, thereby getting more smooth and even textures.

Nozzles. Tips that are used on pastry bags. They come in different shapes and diameters, enabling you to decorate using various forms.

Cupcake liner. Made from paper, it keeps the batter away from the baking mold so as to prevent the dough from sticking to the pan and make it easier for you to take out the cupcakes once they are baked.

Colander. Metallic utensil to sift dry ingredients. They come in various sizes, and they can also help you sprinkle cinnamon, powdered sugar, vanilla powder . . . on the cupcakes.

Ice cream scoop. This tool for scooping out ice cream is also very useful for filling cupcake liners with batter.

Measuring spoons. Set of stainless steel spoons to measure 1 tablespoon (15 ml), 1 teaspoon (5 ml), ½ teaspoon (2.5 ml), and ¼ teaspoon (1.25 ml). In some cases there is also a ⅛ teaspoon included. Makes it very easy for you to measure various quantities specified in recipes.

Spatula. Utensil used to spread creams, especially on cakes, although there are also smaller versions for decorating cupcakes.

Oven. This appliance is where you cook the cupcakes. It usually reaches 425° F (220° C), although for making cupcakes the recommended temperatures are between 330° and 355° F (150° and 180° C). And above all, avoid the grill option, because that could burn the tops of the cupcakes.

Silicone spatula. It helps you get dough or creams out of different containers.

Pastry bag. Plastic or nylon funnel on which nozzles are placed to decorate in different ways.

Cupcake pan. This is a special mold made of silicone or stainless steel with twelve holes where you place the cupcake batter, with or without cupcake liners.

Cooling rack. Metal base that is essential for cooling cupcakes and cakes more quickly.

Rolling pin. Wood or plastic cylinder to stretch dough or fondant for cupcakes.

Measuring cups. Very common in Anglo-Saxon countries, they are often used as an alternative to the scale. One cup equals 250 ml, ½ cup is 125 ml, and ¼ cup is 63 ml.

Food thermometer. For baking, it is recommended that you opt for an alcohol thermometer (made of glass that holds alcohol inside; its volume varies with temperature) or a laser thermometer (allows you to take the temperature of foods without touching the foods themselves).

Whisk. Tool that lets you manually beat batter and cream.

Basic preparations

Throughout this book we will often refer to a number of basic techniques for making cupcakes. Get to know them well so you can get the best results.

Creamy CHEESE

Ingredients

- 13 ounces (375 g) vegan cream cheese
- ¾ stick (85 g) margarine · 1 cup (110 g) powdered sugar · ⅔ cup (150 g) vegetable whipping cream

1. In a bowl, mix the soft margarine (once it is spreadable, a few minutes after taking it out of the refrigerator) and the icing sugar until you get a smooth cream with no lumps.

2. Add the cream cheese and beat it for a few minutes until you get a smooth cream with no lumps. It is important to avoid leaving gobs of cream cheese at the edges or at the bottom of the bowl.

3. Whip the vegetable cream until it is thickened, and add it to the mixture. Continue beating it with a silicone spatula and use it immediately. Otherwise, keep it in the refrigerator until you are ready to use it. However, to use it more easily, warm it slightly in a microwave on low temperature or store it at room temperature for a half hour.

Creamy CHEESE with Maple Syrup

Ingredients
- 13 ounces (375 g) vegan cream cheese
- 1 stick (105 g) margarine · ⅔ cup (150 g) vegetable whipping cream
- 4 ½ tablespoons (90 g) maple syrup

1 In a bowl, mix the soft margarine and the maple syrup until you get a smooth and even cream.

2 Add the cream cheese and beat it for 2 minutes until you get a smooth cream with no lumps, and be careful not to leave gobs of cream cheese at the edges or the bottom of the bowl.

3 Whip the vegetable cream until it is thickened, and add it to the mixture. Continue mixing with a silicone spatula and use it immediately. Otherwise, keep it in the refrigerator until you are ready to use it. However, to use it more easily, warm it slightly in a microwave on low temperature or leave it at room temperature for a half hour.

TOFFEE

Ingredients
• 1 ¼ cups (250 g) brown sugar • ¼ cup
(50 g) glucose (optional) • ¼ teaspoon
salt • ¾ cup (160 g) water • ⅔ cup (150 g)
vegetable cream

1 In a saucepan, mix the brown sugar, glucose, salt, and ⅓ cup (90 g) of water. Place it over medium heat and caramelize the sugar. When it starts to bubble and becomes brownish, remove it from the heat immediately.

2 In another saucepan, mix the vegetable cream and the rest of the water. Place it over medium heat until it starts boiling. Pour the vegetable cream into the saucepan with the caramelized sugar and place over medium heat, stirring it occasionally with a wooden or silicone spoon so the edges do not burn. The toffee is ready when you start to see caramel threads on the spatula.

3 Before using it, store it in a container covered with plastic wrap until it is at room temperature.

MARGARINE
Cream

Ingredients
• 2 sticks (230 g) margarine • 4 cups (475 g) powdered sugar • 2 tablespoons soy milk • extract or essential oil (vanilla, lemon, etc.)

1 In a bowl, mix the soft margarine and half of the powdered sugar and beat it until there are no lumps.

2 Little by little, add the remaining sugar and soy milk, stirring constantly.

3 Add an essential oil and beat it until you get an even, smooth cream that you can season with citrus peel, essential oils, extracts, liquid aromas, nut pastes, freeze-dried fruits, etc.

70 Percent

CHOCOLATE

Cream

Ingredients

• ¾ cup (175 g) vegetable cream • 3 ¾ ounces (105 g) 70 percent chocolate • 1 ⅔ sticks (190 g) margarine • 2 ¾ cups (330 g) powdered sugar • 1 tablespoon vanilla extract

1 Place the vegetable cream in a saucepan over medium heat until it starts boiling. Then, use a bowl and a whisk to mix the boiling cream and chocolate until it is well emulsified. Leave it at room temperature until it reaches approximately 68° F (20° C).

2 In another bowl, mix the soft margarine with half the powdered sugar and beat it until there are no lumps. Gradually, add the remaining sugar and vanilla extract.

3 Lastly, add the chocolate cream mixture and beat it well until it is firm and smooth.

Chocolate MARGARINE Cream

Ingredients
- 1 ½ sticks (170 g) margarine • 2 ounces (60 g) 70 percent chocolate • 4 cups (475 g) powdered sugar • 4 tablespoons soy milk • extract or essential oil (vanilla, lemon, etc.)

1 Melt chocolate in the microwave or double boiler. Before mixing it with the margarine, let it cool a bit so that the margarine does not melt when added.

2 In a bowl, add the soft margarine and melted chocolate. Mix well, add half the powdered sugar, and beat it until there are no lumps.

3 Gradually add the remaining sugar and soy milk, stirring constantly. Add an essential oil and beat it until you get a homogenized cream.

This cream can be seasoned to taste using citrus peel, essential oils, extracts, liquid aromas, paste flavors, freeze-dried fruits, etc.

Caramel ❧
MARGARINE
Cream

Ingredients
• 1 ⅔ sticks (190 g) margarine • 2.8 ounces (80 g) vegan white chocolate • 3 ⅓ cups (405 g) powdered sugar • 3 ounces (90 g) toffee • 2 tablespoons soy milk • 2 teaspoons vanilla extract

1 Melt the white chocolate in the microwave or double boiler. Before mixing it with the margarine, let it cool a bit so that the margarine does not melt when added.

2 In a bowl, add the soft margarine and melted chocolate. Mix well, add half the powdered sugar, and beat it until there are no lumps.

3 Gradually add the remaining sugar, toffee, and soy milk, stirring constantly. Add extract or essential oil and beat it until you get a smooth cream.

SUGAR
Icing/Glaze

Ingredients
- ⅔ cup (150 g) of liquid (water; soy milk; orange, lemon, apple, banana juice . . .)
- 5 cups (600 g) powdered sugar

1 In a bowl, mix the liquid and powdered sugar and beat it vigorously until the frosting has no lumps. Use it to glaze cakes or pastries, or to decorate creams using a pastry bag.

SPARKLING
Chocolate Icing

Ingredients
- ¼ cup (58 g) vegetable cream • ½ cup (128 g) water • ½ cup (116 g) sugar • 1 tablespoon vanilla extract • ½ cup (40 g) cacao powder • 5 ¾ ounces (165 g) 70 percent chocolate • 2 teaspoons (15 g) glucose (optional)

1. In a saucepan, mix the cream, water, sugar, glucose, cacao, and vanilla. Heat the mixture over medium heat and stir well.

2. In another bowl, add the chocolate and when the cacao sauce starts boiling, pour it in slowly. Using a whisk or hand mixer, beat it well until the glaze is well emulsified and without any lumps.

3. Store it in the refrigerator and before using it, melt the glaze using a double boiler or a microwave.

Vegan
WHITE CHOCOLATE
Whipped Cream

Ingredients
- 1 ⅔ cups (400 g) vegetable whipping cream
- 3 tablespoons (40 g) water • 1 vanilla pod
- 7.4 ounces (210 g) vegan white chocolate

1 In a saucepan, mix the cream and water. Cut the vanilla pod in half and scrape out the seeds with the tip of a knife. Add the seeds and pod to the pan. Place it over low heat until it starts boiling. Continue heating it for a couple of minutes so that the vanilla and cream can blend well. Set aside.

2 In a bowl, add the white chocolate. Pour the cream slowly over the chocolate. Using a whisk or hand mixer, beat the mixture well until there are no lumps and the emulsion is perfect.

3 Store the whipped cream in the refrigerator for a day before using it. When ready to use, whip the cream with a wire whisk and use it immediately.

Creamy
CHEESE and
50 Percent Chocolate

Ingredients
- 1 ⅓ cups (305 g) vegan cream cheese
- ½ stick (65 g) margarine • 1 cup (110 g) powdered sugar • 3.3 ounces (95 g) 50 percent chocolate • ½ cup (160 g) vegetable whipping cream

1 Melt the chocolate in a double boiler or in the microwave and leave it at room temperature until it is slightly cool but still retains its liquid texture. Mix soft margarine and sugar until you get a smooth cream with no lumps.

2 Add the melted chocolate to the margarine and sugar. Beat it well. Add the cream cheese and beat it for 2 minutes until there are no lumps or gobs of cream at the edges or bottom.

3 Whip the vegetable cream and add it to the cheese and chocolate mix. Use a spatula to mix it well and use it immediately. Otherwise, store the cream in the refrigerator until you are ready to use. For easier application, warm it slightly in the microwave at low temperature or leave it at room temperature for half an hour.

70 Percent
CHOCOLATE
Shortbread

Ingredients
• 1 cup (204 g) brown sugar • 1 ⅔ sticks (190 g) margarine • 1 ¾ cups (216 g) wheat flour • ½ cup (36 g) cacao powder • ¼ teaspoon salt • ½ teaspoon baking soda • 7.3 ounces (208 g) 70 percent chocolate • 1 tablespoon vanilla extract

1 In a bowl, beat margarine and sugar. In another bowl, mix the flour, cacao, salt, and baking soda. Store the chocolate in the refrigerator for at least 2 hours. Then grind it finely until it has the texture of powder, making sure that it does not melt.

2 Add the flour mixture to the margarine and sugar mix. Knead it until the flour is fully incorporated. Add the crushed chocolate and vanilla extract. Knead the dough lightly, just until it comes together. Be mindful not to overwork the dough. You won't achieve a flaky texture if you overwork it.

3 Roll the dough and cut it into slices. Line the baking sheet with baking paper, place the slices of dough on it, and bake at 325° F (170° C) for about 8 minutes.

DIAMOND SHORTBREAD

Ingredients
- 2 ⅓ sticks (270 g) margarine • ⅔ cup (120 g) sugar • ⅓ teaspoon (1.8 g) salt
- 1 tablespoon vanilla extract • 3 cups (385 g) wheat flour • sugar

1 In a bowl, beat margarine and sugar. Add the flour, vanilla, and salt. Knead the ingredients to mix well, but briefly so that the shortbread has a sandy texture.

2 Cover the dough in plastic wrap and store it in the refrigerator for at least 2 hours. Roll the dough and cut it into slices.

3 In a bowl, coat the shortbread with plenty of sugar, line the baking pan with baking paper, place the slices of dough on it, and bake at 325° F (170° C) for 7 minutes or until edges are slightly browned.

Quick and
CREAMY
Raspberry Marmalade

Ingredients
- ¾ cup (250 g) raspberry sauce • ⅓ cup (80 g) water • 1 cup (200 g) sugar
- 2 ½ teaspoons (5 g) agar

1 In a saucepan, mix all ingredients until the agar is completely dissolved. Place it over medium heat until it starts boiling.

2 Pour it into a glass blender and store it in the refrigerator until well gelled.

3 Grind the jelly until you get a smooth marmalade. Instead of a raspberry sauce, you may use any fruit juice or pulp, adding more water as needed if the fruit is too thick.

Vegan Cupcakes

CHOCOLATE and Banana Cupcakes

Ingredients YIELDS 12

• 1 ¾ cups (230 g) flour • ¾ cup (70 g) cacao • 1 cup (220 g) sugar • 2 teaspoons baking powder • ½ teaspoon baking soda • ½ teaspoon salt • 1 banana • 1 teaspoon vanilla extract • 6.5 ounces (200 g) soy milk • ⅔ cup (130 g) sunflower oil

Decoration:
3 cups (720 g) creamy cheese and 50 percent chocolate (see basic recipe on p. 28) • 1 banana • sugar

1 In a bowl, mix all dry ingredients (flour, sugar, cacao, baking soda, salt, and baking powder). Peel the banana and cut it into cubes that are ⅜ inch wide (1 cm). Add the soy milk, oil, vanilla extract, and banana. Beat it using a wire whip.

Use the batter to fill each cupcake liner halfway.

2 Bake at 355° F (180° C) for approximately 24 minutes, and take them out when a toothpick inserted in the center of each cupcake comes out clean. Store them in a cool place for a couple of hours

3 To make the decoration, peel and cut the banana into slices. Heat a little sugar in a pan and caramelize it over low heat. Add the banana slices in a single layer and let them caramelize on both sides for a few seconds. Remove and set aside.

4 Decorate each cupcake with creamy cheese and 50 percent chocolate and top them off with a banana slice. Store them in the refrigerator for a couple of hours.

MATCHA TEA Cupcakes with Chocolate Whipped Cream

Ingredients YIELDS 12
- 2 cups (270 g) flour • 2 tablespoons (30 g) green matcha tea • 1 cup (200 g) sugar
- 2 teaspoons baking powder • ½ teaspoon baking soda • ½ teaspoon salt • 1 teaspoon vanilla extract • 7.25 ounces (220 g) soy milk
- ⅔ cup (130 g) sunflower oil

Decoration:
- 1 ⅔ cups (410 g) vegetable cream
- 2.5 ounces (70 g) 50 percent chocolate
- 2 ½ cups (30 g) sugar

1 In a bowl, mix all dry ingredients (flour, sugar, baking soda, salt, tea, and baking powder). Add the soy milk, vanilla extract, and oil. Whisk them using a wire whisk. Use the batter to fill each cupcake liner halfway.

2 Bake at 355° F (180° C) for approximately 18 minutes, and take them out when a toothpick inserted in the center of each cupcake comes out clean. Store them in a cool place for a couple of hours.

3 To make the decoration, heat the vegetable cream and sugar to simmer until it starts boiling. Pour the cream into a bowl and add the chocolate. Mix well until you get a smooth cream with no lumps and store it in the refrigerator for 4 hours until chilled. Whip the cream and decorate each cupcake.

ORANGE and Licorice Cupcakes

Ingredients YIELDS 12
· 2 ½ cups (300 g) flour · 1 cup (220 g) sugar · 2 teaspoons baking powder · ½ teaspoon baking soda · ½ teaspoon salt · 1 orange · 6.75 ounces (200 g) water · ⅔ cup (150 g) sunflower oil

Decoration:
· 3 cups (720 g) creamy cheese (see recipe on p. 18) · 2 tablespoons licorice paste · orange peel

1 In a bowl, mix all dry ingredients (flour, sugar, baking soda, salt, and baking powder). Grate the orange peel in the same bowl and add the water, oil, and orange peel. Whip using a wire whisk.

Use the batter to fill each cupcake liner halfway.

2 Bake at 355° F (180° C) for approximately 25 minutes, and take them out when a toothpick inserted in the center of each cupcake comes out clean. Store them in a cool place for a couple of hours.

3 To make the decoration, mix the creamy cheese and the licorice paste. Decorate each cupcake with creamy cheese and licorice, and then sprinkle each one with a little orange peel on top.

COCONUT
Cupcakes

Ingredients YIELDS 12
- 2 ½ cups (300 g) flour • 1 cup (220 g) sugar • 2 teaspoons baking powder • ½ teaspoon baking soda • ½ teaspoon salt • 2 tablespoons coconut • 1 teaspoon vanilla extract • 6.75 ounces (200 g) water • ⅔ cup (150 g) sunflower oil

Balls:
- ½ cup shredded coconut • ½ cup almond flour • ¼ cup agave syrup • ¼ cup coconut oil • grated coconut for the coating

Decoration:
- 3 cups (720 g) creamy cheese (see recipe on p. 18) • grated coconut • 12 coconut balls

1 In a bowl, mix all dry ingredients (flour, sugar, baking soda, salt, coconut, and baking powder). Add vanilla extract, water, and sunflower oil. Stir to combine. Use the batter to fill each cupcake liner halfway.

2 Bake at 355° F (180° C) for approximately 25 minutes, and take them out when a toothpick inserted in the center of each cupcake comes out clean. Store them in a cool place for a couple of hours.

3 To make the balls, heat coconut oil in a double boiler to melt. In a bowl, mix the shredded coconut, almond flour, agave syrup, and coconut oil until you have a smooth and compact dough. Make small balls with the dough and coat them with grated coconut. Store them in the refrigerator for a couple of hours before using.

4 Decorate each cupcake with creamy cheese and store them in the refrigerator. In a hot pan, roast the grated coconut, then place it in a long plate. Decorate each cupcake with a handful of toasted coconut and top them with a coconut ball.

PUMPKIN and Walnut Cupcakes

Ingredients YIELDS 12

· 2 ½ cups (300 g) flour · 1 cup (220 g) sugar · 2 teaspoons baking powder · ½ teaspoon baking soda · ½ teaspoon salt · 1 teaspoon cinnamon · 4 ounces (120 g) soy milk · ¾ cup (210 g) pumpkin (½ cup [130 g] for cake and ¼ cup [80 g] for cream) · ⅔ cup (150 g) sunflower oil · ¾ cup (70 g) walnuts

Decoration:
· 3 cups (720 g) creamy cheese (see recipe on p. 18) · ⅓ cup (80 g) cooked pumpkin · walnuts · nutmeg

1 In a bowl, mix all dry ingredients (flour, sugar, baking soda, salt, cinnamon, and baking powder). Chop ¾ cup (210 g) of pumpkin into cubes and boil separately, ½ cup (130 g) for the cake and ¼ cup (80 g) for the cream, until they are very tender. Strain and set aside separately. Puree ½ cup (130 g) of cooked pumpkin and leave at room temperature. Shred ⅓ cup (80 g) of pumpkin. Chop the walnuts into small pieces. Add soy milk, pumpkin puree, and oil to the bowl with the dry ingredients. Whip using a wire whisk. Add the nuts and stir well. Use the batter to fill each cupcake liner halfway.

2 Bake at 355° F (180° C) for approximately 28 minutes, and take them out when a toothpick inserted in the center of each cupcake comes out clean. Store them in a cool place for a couple of hours. Mix the creamy cheese and the shredded pumpkin.

3 Decorate each cupcake with creamy cheese and pumpkin, top them with a few nuts, and grate a little nutmeg.

PEAR and Maple Syrup Cupcakes

Ingredients YIELDS 12
· 2 ½ cups (300 g) flour · 1 cup (220 g) sugar · 2 teaspoons baking powder · ½ teaspoon baking soda · ½ teaspoon salt · 1 Conference pear · 1 teaspoon vanilla extract · 5.25 ounces (160 g) soy milk · ⅔ cup (150 g) sunflower oil

Compote:
· 1 Conference pear · 1 cup (125 g) blueberries · 6 dried apricots · ½ cup (70 g) raisins · ½ teaspoon cinnamon · 1 tablespoon Cointreau · 6 ½ tablespoons (80 g) sugar

Decoration:
· 3 cups (720 g) creamy cheese with maple syrup (see recipe on p. 19) · pear and blueberry compote

1. Mix all dry ingredients in a bowl (flour, sugar, baking soda, salt, and baking powder). Peel and cut the pear into cubes that are ⅜ inch (1 cm) wide. Cover with water in a saucepan and cook for 2 minutes over low heat. Strain and leave at room temperature. Add soy milk, oil, and vanilla extract to the bowl with dry ingredients. Whip using a wire whisk. Add the diced pear and continue whipping until the pear mixes with the batter.

Use the batter to fill each cupcake liner halfway.

2. Bake at 355° F (180° C) for approximately 25 minutes, and take them out when a toothpick inserted in the center of each cupcake comes out clean. Store them in a cool place for a couple of hours.

3. To make the compote, peel and cut the pear into cubes that are ⅜ inch (1 cm) wide. Chop the apricots and raisins into small pieces. Place the diced pears, blueberries, raisins, dried apricots, sugar, liqueur, and cinnamon in a saucepan. Cook over low heat for 10 minutes, stir occasionally, and make sure that the mixture does not stick and the blueberries do not get crushed. Store it in the refrigerator until the sauce reaches a warm temperature.

4. Decorate each cupcake with creamy cheese with maple syrup, leaving a hole in the middle to fill with some pear and blueberry compote. Store them in the refrigerator for 2 hours before serving.

STRUDELS

Ingredients YIELDS 12

3 apples · 1 cup (180 g) sugar · ⅔ cup (90 g) raisins · ⅓ cup (70 g) rum · ⅔ cup (160 g) water · 1 lemon · 1 teaspoon cinnamon · puff pastry · oil · sugar

Decoration:
1 ¼ cups (300 g) vegetable cream · cinnamon powder · cinnamon sticks

1 Peel the apples, remove the cores, and cut into cubes that are ⅜ inch (1 cm) wide. Place them in a bowl. Boil ½ cup (100 g) of sugar, rum, water, and raisins. Continue simmering for 10 more minutes. Strain raisins and add them to the bowl of apples. Grate the lemon peel and add it to the bowl. Add the remaining sugar and cinnamon. Stir until well blended.

2 Cut the puff pastry into several squares. Place a piece inside each mold, be sure not to break the edges, and cover well. Pour the apple mixture and close with the remaining puff pastry dough. Brush with a little oil and sprinkle some sugar on top.

3 Bake at 375° F (190° C) for approximately 35 minutes, until the pastry is nicely browned. Leave the pastry at room temperature and remove from the mold when they are a little less hot.

4 Whip the cream using a whisk or a blender. Decorate each cupcake with whipped cream, a cinnamon stick, and a little cinnamon powder.

ICED CARAMEL LATTE

Ingredients YIELDS 12

- 2 ½ cups (300 g) flour • 1 cup (220 g) sugar • 2 teaspoons baking powder
- ½ teaspoon baking soda • ½ teaspoon salt
- 1 teaspoon vanilla extract • ¾ cup (180 g) soy milk • ½ cup (110 g) sunflower oil

Coffee topping:
- 5 tablespoons instant coffee • 1 ⅔ cups (400 g) water

Decoration:
- 1 ¾ cups (350 g) vegetable whipping cream • 1 tablespoon ground coffee
- toffee

1 In a bowl, mix all dry ingredients (flour, sugar, baking soda, salt, and baking powder). Add the soy milk, oil, and vanilla extract. Whip using a wire whisk.

Use the batter to fill each cupcake liner halfway.

2 Bake at 355° F (180° C) for approximately 22 minutes, and take them out when a toothpick inserted in the center of each cupcake comes out clean. Store in a cool place for 2 hours.

3 To make the coffee topping, boil the water with instant coffee. Remove pan from the heat and stir well so that the coffee gets dissolved. Carefully cut the tops of the cupcakes and soak each piece with coffee. Store in the freezer for 30 minutes.

4 Whip the vegetable cream with ground coffee and decorate each cupcake. Pour toffee over as needed.

MATCHA TEA and Sesame Cupcakes

Ingredients YIELDS 12

· 2 cups (270 g) flour · 2 tablespoons (30 g) green matcha tea · 1 cup (200 g) sugar · 2 teaspoons baking powder · ½ teaspoon baking soda · ½ teaspoon salt · 1 teaspoon vanilla extract · 1 cup (220 g) soy milk · ⅔ cup (130 g) sunflower oil · sesame seeds

Decoration:

· 3 cups (720 g) creamy cheese (see recipe on p. 18) · green matcha tea

1. In a bowl, mix all dry ingredients (flour, tea, sugar, baking soda, salt, and baking powder). Add the soy milk, vanilla extract, and oil. Whip using a wire whisk. Place a teaspoon of sesame seeds in each cupcake liner. Then use the batter to fill each cupcake liner halfway.

2. Bake at 355° F (180° C) for approximately 18 minutes, and take them out when a toothpick inserted in the center of each cupcake comes out clean. Store them in a cool place for a couple of hours.

3. Decorate each cupcake with creamy cheese, then sprinkle matcha green tea on top.

VANILLA and White Chocolate Cupcakes

Ingredients YIELDS 12

· 1 ⅔ cups (200 g) flour · 1 cup (220 g) sugar · 2 teaspoons baking powder · ½ teaspoon baking soda · ½ teaspoon salt · 1 teaspoon vanilla extract · ¾ cup (180 g) soy milk · ¾ cup (105 g) cornstarch · ½ cup (110 g) sunflower oil · 3.5 ounces (100 g) vegan white chocolate

Rum topping:
· ½ cup (100 g) water · ⅓ cup (70 g) rum · ½ cup (100 g) sugar · 1 vanilla pod

Decoration:
· 10 cups (600 g) vegan white chocolate whipped cream (see recipe on p. 27) · vanilla powder · 3.5 ounces (100 g) vegan white chocolate

1 In a bowl, mix the dry ingredients. Chop the chocolate into cubes that are ⅜ inch (1 cm) wide. In another bowl, dilute the cornstarch with milk and add the oil and vanilla extract. Beat with a whisk. Add the chocolate and stir. Use the batter to fill each cupcake liner halfway.

2 Bake at 355° F (180° C) for approximately 26 minutes, and take them out when a toothpick inserted in the center of each cupcake comes out clean. Store them in a cool place for a couple of hours.

3 To make the rum topping, heat the water, rum, and sugar. Cut the vanilla pod in half, take out the seeds, and place them in the saucepan along with the pod. Cook until it starts to boil and strain the mixture. Cut the tops of the cupcakes and soak them with rum. Store them in the refrigerator for 1 hour.

4 To make the decoration, melt the chocolate in a double boiler and pour it over a sheet of parchment paper. Let it sit for 10 minutes in the refrigerator and cut it into pieces. Place it in the refrigerator for 30 minutes. Decorate each cupcake with whipped cream, vanilla powder, and a piece of white chocolate.

TOFFEE DELIGHT

Ingredients YIELDS 12
· 2 ½ cups (300 g) flour · 1 cup (180 g) brown sugar · 2 teaspoons baking powder · ½ teaspoon baking soda · ½ teaspoon salt · 1 teaspoon vanilla extract · 1.75 ounces (50 g) toffee · 6.5 ounces (200 g) soy milk · ⅔ cup (150 g) sunflower oil

Decoration:
· 3 ounces (80 g) toffee (for cream cheese) · 3 cups (720 g) creamy cheese (see recipe on p. 18) · toffee · diamond shortbread

1 In a bowl, mix all dry ingredients (flour, sugar, baking soda, salt, and baking powder). Add the soy milk, toffee, oil, and vanilla extract. Whip using a wire whisk. Use the batter to fill each cupcake liner halfway.

2 Bake at 355° F (180° C) for approximately 25 minutes, and take them out when a toothpick inserted in the center of each cupcake comes out clean. Store them in a cool place for a couple of hours.

3 Mix 3 ounces (80 g) of toffee with creamy cheese and decorate each cupcake. Use your fingers to break a few pieces of diamond shortbread and sprinkle them over each cupcake. Finish decorating with some toffee.

TIRAMISU
Cupcakes

Ingredients YIELDS 12
• 2 ½ cups (300 g) flour • 1 cup (220 g) sugar • 2 teaspoons baking powder • ½ teaspoon baking soda • ½ teaspoon salt • 1 teaspoon vanilla extract • ¾ cup (180 g) soy milk • ½ cup (110 g) sunflower oil

Coffee topping:
• 5 tablespoons instant coffee • 6.75 ounces (200 g) water • 3 tablespoons (40 g) amaretto • ¾ cup (150 g) sugar

Decoration:
• 1 cup (250 g) vegetable whipping cream • 1 cup (250 g) vegan cream cheese • 2 tablespoons amaretto • 1 tablespoon ground coffee • cacao powder • 70 percent chocolate shortbread

1 In a bowl, mix all dry ingredients (flour, sugar, baking soda, salt, and baking powder). Add the soy milk, oil, and vanilla extract. Whip using a wire whisk. Use the batter to fill each cupcake liner halfway.

2 Bake at 355° F (180° C) for approximately 28 minutes, and take them out when a toothpick inserted in the center of each cupcake comes out clean. Store them in a cool place for a couple of hours.

3 To make the coffee topping, boil water, amaretto, sugar, and instant coffee. Remove from heat and stir until coffee is dissolved. Carefully cut off the tops of the cupcakes and set them aside. Soak the rest with coffee topping and store them in the refrigerator for 2 hours.

4 For the decoration, beat the cream cheese until fluffy, then slowly add the vegetable cream, ensuring that there are no lumps. Add the ground coffee and amaretto. Continue beating until it becomes a smooth cream. Decorate each cupcake with a little cream, then put each top back on, and top with more cream. Using a strainer, sprinkle each piece with cacao powder and a few pieces of 70 percent chocolate shortbread that you previously broke into pieces with your fingers.

SACHERTORTE
Cupcakes

Ingredients YIELDS 12

2 cups (200 g) flour · ½ cup (40 g) cacao · 1 cup (220 g) sugar · ½ cup (40 g) almond flour · 2 teaspoons baking powder · ½ teaspoon baking soda · ½ teaspoon salt · 1 teaspoon vanilla extract · 6.5 ounces (200 g) soy milk · ½ cup (110 g) sunflower oil

Decoration:

shiny chocolate glaze · 1 ¼ cups (300 g) vegetable whipping cream · apricot marmalade

1 In a bowl, mix all dry ingredients (flour, sugar, cacao, almond flour, baking soda, salt, and baking powder). Add the soy milk, oil, and vanilla extract. Whip using a wire whisk. Use the batter to fill each cupcake liner halfway.

2 Bake at 355° F (180° C) for approximately 22 minutes, and take them out when a toothpick inserted in the center of each cupcake comes out clean. Store them in a cool place for a couple of hours.

3 Slice each cupcake horizontally three times. Melt the chocolate glaze and use it to decorate the inside of the top slice of each cupcake. Spread a little apricot marmalade in the other two sections and place atop each cupcake. Store them in the refrigerator for 1 hour. Whip the vegetable cream and decorate each cupcake.

ISPAHAN
Cupcakes

Ingredients YIELDS 12

- 1 ¾ cups (200 g) digestive biscuits
- 1 stick (100 g) margarine • 1 teaspoon cinnamon • 1 ⅓ cups (300 g) cream cheese
- 2 tablespoons (15 g) wheat flour • ½ cup (90 g) sugar • 2 ½ tablespoons (40 g) vegetable cream • 3 lychees • 1 tablespoon rosewater • ⅓ cup (45 g) cornstarch
- ½ cup (100 g) water

Decoration:
- ¾ cup (200 g) vegetable cream
- 1 teaspoon rosewater • raspberries

1 Crush the biscuits and mix with margarine and cinnamon. Distribute equally between the cupcake molds.

In a bowl, mix the flour and sugar. In another bowl, beat the cheese and gradually add the mixture. Cut the lychees into small cubes. Dilute the cornstarch with water, rosewater, and cream. Slowly add this mixture and chopped lychees to the cheese. Continue beating. Pour the batter in each cupcake liner.

2 Bake at 300° F (150° C) for 1 hour in a water bath. Remove and keep it in the fridge for 3 hours before taking out of the mold.

3 Whip the cream with rosewater and decorate each cupcake. Place the raspberries around the cream and, as an option, garnish with rose petals.

RED VELVET
Cupcakes

Ingredients YIELDS 12
• 2 ⅓ cups (290 g) flour • 2 tablespoons
(10 g) cacao • 1 cup (220 g) sugar
• 2 teaspoons baking powder • ½ teaspoon
baking soda • ½ teaspoon salt • red food
coloring • 2 teaspoons vanilla extract
• 6.5 ounces (200 g) soy milk • ⅔ cup (150 g)
sunflower oil

Decoration:
• 3 cups (720 g) creamy cheese (see recipe
on p. 18) • 12 cherries • 3.5 ounces (100 g)
vegan white chocolate

1 In a bowl, mix all dry ingredients (flour, sugar, cacao, baking soda, salt, and baking powder). Add the soy milk, oil, food coloring, and vanilla extract. Whip using a wire whisk. Use the batter to fill each cupcake liner halfway.

2 Bake at 355° F (180° C) for approximately 24 minutes, and take them out when a toothpick inserted in the center of each cupcake comes out clean. Store in a cool place for 2 hours.

3 Melt vegan white chocolate in a double boiler. Cover each cherry with melted chocolate. Place the fruit on a plate lined with baking parchment paper and store them in the refrigerator for 1 hour. Decorate each cupcake with creamy cheese and 1 cherry dipped in white chocolate.

CHEESECAKE and Pumpkin Cupcakes

Ingredients YIELDS 12
- 1 ¾ cups (200 g) digestive biscuits
- 1 stick (100 g) margarine • 1 teaspoon cinnamon • 1 ¼ cups (300 g) vegan cream cheese • 2 tablespoons (15 g) wheat flour
- ½ cup (90 g) sugar • 2 ½ tablespoons (40 g) vegetable cream • 1 orange • ⅓ cup (45 g) cornstarch • ⅔ cup (150 g) pumpkin
- ¼ teaspoon cinnamon • a pinch of nutmeg
- a pinch of ground cloves • a pinch of cardamom

Decoration:
- 1 cup (250 g) vegetable cream • 3 ounces (80 g) toffee

1 Peel and cut pumpkin into cubes. Boil until it is tender. Store in a cool place.

Crush the biscuits and mix with margarine and cinnamon. Place in the mold.

In a bowl, mix the flour and sugar. In another bowl, beat the cheese, and gradually add the mixture. Grate the orange peel and mix with cream, diced pumpkin, cinnamon, cardamom, nutmeg, cloves, and cornstarch. Gradually add this mixture to the cheese and continue beating. Pour the batter into each cupcake liner.

2 Bake at 300° F (150° C) for 1 hour in a water bath. Store them in the refrigerator for 3 hours before taking them out of the mold.

3 Whip and mix the cream with pre-melted toffee and decorate each cupcake. Sprinkle with a little cinnamon.

PISTACHIO and Raspberry Cupcakes

Ingredients YIELDS 12

• 2 ½ cups (300 g) flour • 1 cup (220 g) sugar • 2 teaspoons baking powder • ½ teaspoon baking soda • ½ teaspoon salt • 1 teaspoon vanilla extract • 6.75 ounces (200 g) water • ⅔ cup (130 g) sunflower oil • ¾ cup (100 g) green pistachios

Decoration:
• 10 cups (600 g) vegan white chocolate whipped cream (see recipe on p. 27) • quick and creamy raspberry marmalade (see recipe on p. 31) • pistachios

1 In a bowl, mix all dry ingredients (flour, sugar, baking soda, salt, and baking powder). Mince the pistachios. Add water, oil, vanilla extract, and crushed pistachios to the bowl. Whip using a wire whisk. Use the batter to fill each cupcake liner halfway.

2 Bake at 355° F (180° C) for approximately 24 minutes, and take them out when a toothpick inserted in the center of each cupcake comes out clean. Store them in a cool place for a couple of hours. Using a knife, carve out a hole in each cupcake's top and fill the inside with raspberry marmalade.

3 To make the decoration, mince a few green pistachios. Put a little whipped cream on each cupcake and sprinkle with plenty of crushed pistachios.

DRIED FRUIT and
Maple Syrup Cupcakes

Ingredients YIELDS 12

• 2 cups (270 g) flour • ½ cup (40 g) almond flour • 1 cup (180 g) sugar • 2 teaspoons baking powder • ½ teaspoon baking soda • ½ teaspoon salt • 6.75 ounces (200 g) water • ⅔ cup (130 g) sunflower oil • ¼ cup (30 g) walnuts • ¼ cup (30 g) toasted hazelnuts • ⅓ cup (40 g) raisins • 3 dates

Decoration:

• 3 cups (720 g) creamy cheese (see recipe on p. 18) • maple syrup

1 In a bowl, mix all dry ingredients (flour, almond flour, sugar, baking soda, salt, and baking powder). Chop walnuts, hazelnuts, raisins, and dates in irregular pieces. Add water, oil, hazelnuts, walnuts, raisins, and dates to the bowl. Whip using a wire whisk. Use the batter to fill each cupcake liner halfway.

2 Bake at 355° F (180° C) for approximately 27 minutes, and take them out when a toothpick inserted in the center of each cupcake comes out clean. Store them in a cool place for a couple of hours.

3 Decorate each cupcake with creamy cheese, leaving a hole in the middle to fill with maple syrup. Serve at once.

CHOCOLATE and Passion Fruit Cupcakes

Ingredients YIELDS 12

1 ¾ cups (230 g) flour · 1 cup (70 g) cacao · 1 cup (220 g) sugar · 2 teaspoons baking powder · ½ teaspoon baking soda · ½ teaspoon salt · 1 teaspoon vanilla extract · 6.75 ounces (200 g) water · ½ cup (110 g) sunflower oil · 1 ounce (30 g) 70 percent chocolate

Decoration:
½ cup (100 g) vegetable cream · ¼ cup (50 g) passion fruit juice or pulp · 5 ounces (146 g) 70 percent chocolate · ⅔ cup (150 g) vegetable whipping cream · ½ cup (100 g) water · ½ cup (100 g) sugar · 1 lemon

1 In a bowl, mix all dry ingredients (flour, sugar, cacao, baking soda, salt, and baking powder). Melt the chocolate in a double boiler and mix with the oil. Add the water, the chocolate mixture, and vanilla extract. Whip using a wire whisk. Use this batter to fill each cupcake liner halfway.

2 Bake at 355° F (180° C) for approximately 25 minutes, and take them out when a toothpick inserted in the center of each cupcake comes out clean. Store in a cool place for 8 hours.

3 To make the decoration, cut the lemon peel into thin strips. Boil the water and sugar, add the lemon strips, and let it crystallize for 20 minutes over low heat. Remove from heat and leave at room temperature. Boil ½ cup (100 g) cream with passion fruit. Place the chocolate in a bowl, and pour over the mixture of cream and fruit. Stir with a whisk to make a smooth ganache. Whip and mix ⅔ cup (150 g) whipping cream with the ganache until it has the texture of mousse. Decorate each cupcake with mousse and candied lemon strips.

LIMONCELLO
Cupcakes

Ingredients YIELDS 12
- 2 ½ cups (300 g) flour • 1 cup (220 g)
sugar • 2 teaspoons baking powder
- ½ teaspoon baking soda • ½ teaspoon salt
- 1 lemon • 6.5 ounces (200 g) soy milk
- ⅔ cup (130 g) sunflower oil • limoncello

Decoration:
- 1 ½ cups (350 g) vegetable whipping
cream • ⅓ cup (80 g) limoncello

1 In a bowl, mix all dry ingredients (flour, sugar, baking soda, salt, and baking powder). Grate the lemon peel. Add the soy milk, oil, and grated lemon peel. Whip using a wire whisk.

Use the batter to fill each cupcake liner halfway.

2 Bake at 355° F (180° C) for approximately 24 minutes, and take them out when a toothpick inserted in the center of each cupcake comes out clean. Store them in a cool place for a couple of hours. Cut off the top of each cupcake and set aside. Top each cupcake with a splash of limoncello.

3 Whip the vegetable cream, add the limoncello, and stir with a spatula.

Decorate each cupcake with cream and limoncello, place the tops of the cupcakes back on, and decorate with more whipped cream (optional).

GERMAN CHOCOLATE
Cupcakes

Ingredients YIELDS 12
- 1 ¾ cups (230 g) flour · 1 cup (70 g) cacao · 1 cup (220 g) sugar · 2 teaspoons baking powder · ½ teaspoon baking soda · ½ teaspoon salt · 1 teaspoon vanilla extract · 6.5 ounces (220 g) soy milk · ½ cup (100 g) sunflower oil

Filling:
- 1 cup (200 g) brown sugar · 1 cup (200 g) vegetable cream · ¼ stick (30 g) margarine · 5 ounces (140 g) grated coconut · 1 ⅓ cups (200 g) walnuts

Decoration:
- ¾ cup (200 g) vegetable cream
- 7 ounces (200 g) 70 percent chocolate
- ¾ cup (200 g) vegetable whipping cream to place on top

1. In a bowl, mix all dry ingredients (flour, sugar, cacao, baking soda, salt, and baking powder). Add the soy milk, oil, and vanilla extract. Whip using a wire whisk. Use the batter to fill each cupcake liner halfway.

2. Bake at 355° F (180° C) for approximately 24 minutes, and take them out when a toothpick inserted in the center of each cupcake comes out clean. Store in a cool place for 8 hours.

3. To make the filling, first mince the walnuts with a knife. Boil the cream, brown sugar, margarine, coconut, and chopped walnuts into a dry paste. Store it in the refrigerator for 2 hours. Slice the cupcakes horizontally in half and spread the filling inside. Join both sides and store them in the refrigerator for 1 hour.

4. To decorate the cupcakes, boil ¾ cup (200 g) of cream. Place the chocolate in a bowl, and pour the hot cream over it. Stir with a whisk to make a smooth ganache. Whip the other ¾ cup (200 g) of cream and mix with the ganache until it has the texture of mousse. With a hot spoon, form a quenelle of creamy chocolate mousse to place on top of each cupcake.

STRAWBERRY-TOPPED
Cupcakes

Ingredients YIELDS 12

• 2 ½ cups (300 g) flour • 1 cup (220 g) sugar • 2 teaspoons baking powder • ½ teaspoon baking soda • ½ teaspoon salt • 1 teaspoon vanilla extract • 6.5 ounces (200 g) soy milk • ⅔ cup (130 g) sunflower oil

Strawberry sauce:
• 2 pounds (1 kg) strawberries • 1 cup (200 g) sugar

Decoration:
• 1 ¾ cups (450 g) vegetable whipping cream • strawberries

1 In a bowl, mix all dry ingredients (flour, sugar, baking soda, salt, and baking powder). Add the soy milk, oil, and vanilla extract. Whip using a wire whisk.

Use the batter to fill each cupcake liner halfway.

2 Bake at 355° F (180° C) for approximately 24 minutes, and take them out when a toothpick inserted in the center of each cupcake comes out clean. Store them in a cool place for a couple of hours.

3 To make the strawberry sauce, cut the fruit into pieces, and boil in a saucepan with the sugar. Crush and strain well to remove lumps and seeds. Save it in the refrigerator.

4 To make the decoration, whip the vegetable cream and place it inside a pastry bag. Slice the strawberries. In a soup plate, pour the strawberry sauce and place the cupcake on it. Decorate with cream and sliced strawberries. Serve at once.

CANDIED GINGERBREAD
Cupcakes

Ingredients YIELDS 12
• 2 cups (270 g) flour • ½ cup (50 g) almond flour • ½ cup (100 g) brown sugar • 2 ½ teaspoons baking powder • 1 teaspoon baking soda • ½ teaspoon salt • 2 teaspoons gingerbread mix (ginger, cinnamon, anise, and cardamom) • 1 orange • ½ cup (120 g) agave syrup • ½ cup (120 g) water • ½ cup (100 g) sunflower oil • 3 ounces (85 g) candied ginger

Decoration:
• 3 cups (720 g) creamy cheese (see recipe on p. 18) • candied ginger

1 In a bowl, mix all dry ingredients (flour, almond flour, sugar, baking soda, salt, spices, and baking powder).

Chop candied ginger with a knife. Add water, agave syrup, oil, and chopped candied ginger to the dry mix. Beat with a whisk and use the batter to fill each cupcake liner halfway.

2 Bake at 355° F (180° C) for approximately 27 minutes, and take them out when a toothpick inserted in the center of each cupcake comes out clean. Store them in a cool place for a couple of hours.

3 Decorate each cupcake with creamy cheese and candied ginger.

FERRERO ROCHER
Cupcakes

Ingredients YIELDS 12
• 1 ¾ cups (230 g) flour • ¾ cup (70 g) cacao • 1 cup (220 g) sugar • 2 teaspoons baking powder • ½ teaspoon baking soda • ½ teaspoon salt • 1 teaspoon vanilla extract • 6.5 ounces (200 g) soy milk • ⅔ cup (130 g) sunflower oil

Decoration:
• 1 ¾ cups (450 g) vegetable whipping cream • 14 ounces (400 g) hazelnut praline • gianduja icing (see ingredients below) • gold dust

For gianduja:
• 18 ounces (500 g) 70 percent chocolate • 1 ½ tablespoons (20 g) sunflower oil • 1 cup (140 g) hazelnut paste • ⅓ cup (50 g) hazelnut sprinkles

1 In a bowl, mix all dry ingredients (flour, sugar, cacao, baking soda, salt, and baking powder). Add the soy milk, oil, and vanilla extract. Whip using a wire whisk. Use the batter to fill each cupcake liner halfway.

2 Bake at 355° F (180° C) for approximately 24 minutes, and take them out when a toothpick inserted in the center of each cupcake comes out clean. Store them in a cool place for a couple of hours.

3 Whip the vegetable cream until it is very firm. Add the hazelnut praline and mix carefully. Using a spatula cover each cupcake with this cream. Store in the freezer for at least 5 hours.

4 To make the gianduja, mix chocolate, hazelnut paste, and sunflower oil in a bowl, and then melt it in a double boiler until its texture is smooth. Toast the hazelnut sprinkles, add them to the mixture, and stir. Place the cupcakes on a wire rack and glaze them with the gianduja. Sprinkle them with gold dust and keep them in the refrigerator for 30 minutes before serving.

Berry
CHEESECAKE
Cupcakes

Ingredients YIELDS 12

1 ¾ cups (200 g) digestive biscuits
1 stick (100 g) margarine · 1 teaspoon
cinnamon · 1 ¼ cups (300 g) vegan cream
cheese · 2 tablespoons (15 g) wheat flour
½ cup (90 g) sugar · 3 ⅓ tablespoons
(40 g) cream · 1 lemon · ⅓ cup (45 g)
cornstarch · 7 tablespoons (100 g) water

Decoration:
¾ cup (100 g) raspberries · ¾ cup (100 g)
strawberries · 1.75 ounces (50 g) red
currants · ½ cup (100 g) sugar · ⅔ cup
(150 g) vegetable cream

1 Crush the biscuits and mix with margarine and cinnamon. Distribute this mixture evenly between each mold. In a bowl, mix the flour and ½ cup (90 g) of sugar. Gradually add the cream cheese (previously beaten). Zest the lemon and add it to the water. Add cornstarch and cream. Gradually add this mixture to the cream cheese and continue beating.

Use the batter to fill each cupcake liner halfway.

2 Bake at 300° F (150° C) for 1 hour in a water bath. Store them in the refrigerator for 3 hours before taking them out of the mold.

3 To make the decoration, cut and cook the berries in a saucepan with ½ cup (100 g) sugar for a couple of minutes after it has started to boil. Store the compote in the fridge. Whip the cream and decorate each cupcake, leaving a hole for the compote.

CHOCOLATE AND LIMONCELLO
Cheesecake Cupcakes

Ingredients YIELDS 12
• 1 ¾ cups (200 g) digestive biscuits
• 1 stick (100 g) margarine • 1 ⅓ cups
(300 g) vegan cream cheese • 2 tablespoons
(15 g) wheat flour • ½ cup (90 g) sugar
• 1 teaspoon cinnamon • 2 ½ tablespoons
(40 g) vegetable cream • 1 teaspoon vanilla
extract • ⅓ cup (45 g) cornstarch
• ½ cup (100 g) water • 2 tablespoons (10 g)
cacao

Decoration:
• ¾ cup (200 g) whipping cream
• 3 ounces (80 g) 70 percent chocolate
• ½ cup (120 g) limoncello • chocolate
glaze

1 Crush the biscuits and mix with margarine and cinnamon. Distribute this mixture evenly between each mold. Mix the flour and the sugar. Gradually add the cream cheese (previously beaten). Dilute the cornstarch with the water, vanilla extract, and cream. Gradually add this mixture to the cheese and continue beating.

Divide batter into two parts. With a sieve, add cacao powder to one-half of the batter, making sure that there are no lumps.

Join the two halves of dough and fill each cupcake liner halfway.

2 Bake at 300° F (150° C) for 1 hour in a water bath. Store them in the refrigerator for 3 hours before taking them out of the mold. Melt the chocolate in a double boiler, add the limoncello, and mix with a whisk to make a smooth and even ganache.

3 Whip the cream and add the limoncello ganache. Stir with a spatula until the cream is well mixed. Decorate each cupcake with limoncello cream and add a few drops of chocolate glaze.

STRAWBERRY and Chocolate Cupcakes

Ingredients YIELDS 12
· 2 cups (270 g) flour · ⅓ cup (30 g) cacao · 1 cup (220 g) sugar · 2 teaspoons baking powder · ½ teaspoon baking soda · ½ teaspoon salt · 1 teaspoon vanilla extract · 1 ½ cups (180 g) strawberries · ⅔ cup (130 g) sunflower oil · 3.5 ounces (100 g) 70 percent chocolate

Decoration:
· 10 cups (600 g) vegan white chocolate whipped cream (see recipe on p. 27) · 12 strawberries · 3.5 ounces (100 g) 70 percent chocolate · 1.75 ounces (50 g) vegan white chocolate

1 In a bowl, mix all dry ingredients (flour, sugar, cacao, baking soda, salt, and baking powder). Crush the strawberries and strain them in a colander. Melt the chocolate in a double boiler and mix with the oil. Add the strawberries, oil, melted chocolate, and vanilla extract to the dry ingredients. Whip using a wire whisk.

Use the batter to fill each cupcake liner halfway.

2 Bake at 355° F (180° C) for approximately 24 minutes, and take them out when a toothpick inserted in the center of each cupcake comes out clean. Store them in a cool place for a couple of hours.

3 To make the decoration, top the strawberries with melted chocolate. Place the pieces on a plate lined with baking parchment and store them in the refrigerator for 20 minutes. Melt white chocolate in a double boiler and use a spoon to draw small strips over the strawberries. Store it in the fridge for 20 minutes. Decorate each cupcake with whipped cream and top off with a glazed strawberry.

ALMOND and
White Chocolate Cupcakes

Ingredients YIELDS 12

- 1 ¾ cups (230 g) flour · ¾ cup (70 g) cacao · 1 cup (220 g) sugar · 2 teaspoons baking powder · ½ teaspoon baking soda · ½ teaspoon salt · 1 teaspoon vanilla extract · 6.5 ounces (200 g) soy milk · ⅔ cup (130 g) sunflower oil · ¾ cup (120 g) Marcona almonds

Decoration:
- 3 cups (720 g) creamy cheese (see recipe on p. 18) · 3.5 ounces (100 g) vegan white chocolate · 2 cups (200 g) slivered almonds

1 In a bowl, mix all dry ingredients (flour, sugar, cacao, baking soda, salt, and baking powder). Chop the almonds with a knife and add them to a bowl. Add the soy milk, oil, and vanilla extract. Whip using a wire whisk. Use the batter to fill each cupcake liner halfway.

2 Bake at 355° F (180° C) for approximately 24 minutes, and take them out when a toothpick inserted in the center of each cupcake comes out clean. Store them in a cool place for a couple of hours.

3 To make the decoration, toast slivered almonds in the oven at 400° F (200° C) for 8 to 15 minutes, removing when they are a golden color. Leave at room temperature. Place the melted white chocolate in a pastry bag with a narrow nozzle. Using a spatula, decorate each cupcake with creamy cheese.

Coat with slivered almonds. Using the pastry bag, apply the chocolate on top of the creamy cheese and store them in the refrigerator for 2 hours before serving.

RASPBERRY and
Whiskey Cupcakes

Ingredients YIELDS 12
· 2 ½ cups (300 g) flour · 1 cup (220 g) sugar · 2 teaspoons baking powder · ½ teaspoon baking soda · ½ teaspoon salt · 1 teaspoon vanilla extract · ¾ cup (200 g) almond milk · ⅔ cup (130 g) sunflower oil · ¾ cup (100 g) raspberries

Decoration:
· 10 cups (600 g) vegan white chocolate whipped cream (see recipe on p. 27) · 4 ⅓ tablespoons (70 g) whiskey · raspberry marmalade

1 In a bowl, mix all dry ingredients (flour, sugar, baking soda, salt, and baking powder). Add almond milk, oil, and vanilla extract. Whip using a wire whisk. Add raspberries and mix carefully to prevent breakage. Use the batter to fill each cupcake liner halfway.

2 Bake at 355° F (180° C) for approximately 20 minutes, and take them out when a toothpick inserted in the center of each cupcake comes out clean. Store them in a cool place for a couple of hours. Make a hole in the top of each cupcake and fill the inside with raspberry marmalade.

3 Using a spatula mix the vegan white chocolate whipped cream and whiskey. Decorate each cupcake with this mixture.

APPLE and Lemon Cupcakes

Ingredients YIELDS 12

· 2 ½ cups (300 g) flour · 1 cup (220 g) sugar · 2 teaspoons baking powder · ½ teaspoon baking soda · ½ teaspoon salt · ¾ cup (200 g) apple juice · ⅔ cup (130 g) sunflower oil · 1 Golden apple · 1 lemon

Decoration:
· 1 ½ cups (350 g) vegetable whipping cream · ½ cup (60 g) powdered sugar · 1 lemon · 1 Golden apple

1 In a bowl, mix all dry ingredients (flour, sugar, baking soda, salt, and baking powder). Peel, core, and cut the apple into ⅜-inch (1 cm) cubes. Grate the lemon peel. Add apple juice, lemon peel, oil, and apple cubes to the bowl. Whip using a wire whisk. Use the batter to fill each cupcake liner halfway.

2 Bake at 355° F (180° C) for approximately 30 minutes, and take them out when a toothpick inserted in the center of each cupcake comes out clean. Store them in a cool place for a couple of hours.

3 Whip the vegetable cream with the powdered sugar. Add lemon juice and mix using a spatula, careful not to lose the cream. Decorate each cupcake with whipped cream and thin apple wedges.

BLUEBERRY
Cupcakes

Ingredients YIELDS 12
· 2 ½ cups (300 g) flour · 1 cup (220 g)
sugar · 2 teaspoons baking powder
· ½ teaspoon baking soda · ½ teaspoon
salt · ½ teaspoon cinnamon · 1 teaspoon
vanilla extract · 6.5 ounces (200 g) soy
milk · ⅔ cup (130 g) sunflower oil
· 1 lemon · 1 cup (125 g) blueberries

Decoration:
· 1 ½ cups (360 g) creamy cheese (see
recipe on p. 18) · 12 blueberries

1 In a bowl, mix all dry ingredients (flour, sugar, baking soda, salt, cinnamon, and baking powder). Grate the lemon peel. Add to bowl the soy milk, lemon peel, oil, and vanilla extract. Whip using a wire whisk. Add the blueberries and stir carefully to prevent breakage.

Use the batter to fill each cupcake liner halfway. Sprinkle with sugar.

2 Bake at 355° F (180° C) for approximately 24 minutes, and take them out when a toothpick inserted in the center of each cupcake comes out clean. Store them in a cool place for a couple of hours.

3 Decorate each cupcake with creamy cheese and one blueberry on top.

CARROT and Raisin Cupcakes

Ingredients
· 1 ⅓ cups (170 g) flour · ⅔ cup (130 g) brown sugar · 1 teaspoon baking powder · ½ teaspoon baking soda · ½ teaspoon salt · 5 ounces (150 g) peeled carrot · 1 teaspoon cinnamon · 7 tablespoons (100 g) water · 6 ½ tablespoons (90 g) sunflower oil · ¾ cup (100 g) raisins

Decoration:
· 3 cups (720 g) creamy cheese (see recipe on p. 18) · cinnamon

1 In a bowl, mix all dry ingredients (flour, sugar, baking soda, salt, baking powder, and cinnamon). Mince the carrot. In a saucepan, boil raisins and simmer for 10 minutes. Strain and mince with a food processor or hand blender.

Add water, oil, chopped carrots, and chopped raisins to the dry ingredients. Whip using a wire whisk. Use the batter to fill each cupcake liner halfway.

2 Bake at 355° F (180° C) for approximately 30 minutes, and take them out when a toothpick inserted in the center of each cupcake comes out clean. Store them in a cool place for a couple of hours.

3 Decorate each cupcake with creamy cheese and sprinkle with a little cinnamon.

PIÑA COLADA
Cupcakes

Ingredients YIELDS 12
• 1 ⅔ cups (200 g) flour · 1 cup (220 g)
brown sugar · 1 teaspoon baking powder
· 1 ½ teaspoons baking soda · ½ teaspoon
salt · 1 teaspoon vanilla extract · 1 cup
(120 g) cornstarch · ½ cup (120 g)
coconut milk · ½ cup (100 g) pineapple
juice · ⅔ cup (150 g) sunflower oil

Rum topping:
· ½ cup (100 g) sugar · ¾ cup (175 g)
water · 2 ½ tablespoons (40 g) rum

Decoration:
· 10 ounces (250 g) diced pineapple
· ¼ cup (40 g) brown sugar · 2 tablespoons
grated coconut · 1 tablespoon rum
· 2 ½ cups (600 g) creamy cheese (see
recipe on p. 18)

1 In a bowl, mix all dry ingredients (flour, sugar, baking soda, salt, and baking powder).

In another bowl, mix the cornstarch, coconut milk, and pineapple juice. Add them to the bowl of dry ingredients, together with the oil and vanilla extract. Whip using a wire whisk. Use the batter to fill each cupcake liner halfway.

2 To prepare the syrup, in a saucepan over medium heat place the rum, sugar, and water. Let it boil, remove from heat, and store covered.

3 Bake at 355° F (180° C) for approximately 21 minutes, and take them out when a toothpick inserted in the center of each cupcake comes out clean. Store them in a cool place for a couple of hours. Cut off a piece of each cupcake top and soak it in rum syrup. Store in a cool place.

4 In a skillet, heat the brown sugar, rum, coconut, and half the pineapple cubes. Let the sugar dissolve completely, remove from heat, and mix with the rest of the diced pineapple. Store in a cool place for 1 hour. Decorate each cupcake with creamy cheese but leave a hole in the middle to fill with pineapple cubes.

Mini
STRAWBERRY AND VIOLET
Plum Cakes

Ingredients YIELDS 12

· 2 ½ cups (305 g) flour · 1 cup (215 g) brown sugar · ½ teaspoon baking soda · 2 teaspoons baking powder · ½ teaspoon salt · 1 teaspoon vanilla extract · ¼ cup (50 g) fresh strawberries · 6.5 ounces (200 g) soy milk · ½ cup (115 g) sunflower oil

Decoration:

· 1 ¼ cups (200 g) chocolate fondant (not the kind used for covering cakes, but the classic French pastry chocolate fondant that is wetter and less compact) · red food coloring · 1 ¼ cups (300 g) vegetable whipping cream · ¼ teaspoon (1 g) violet essential oil · lilac coloring

1 In a bowl, mix all dry ingredients (flour, sugar, baking soda, salt, and baking powder). Cut the strawberries into small cubes. Add the soy milk, oil, and vanilla extract to bowl. Whip using a wire whisk. Add strawberries and stir carefully to prevent them from breaking apart. Use the dough to fill each plum cake liner halfway.

2 Bake at 355° F (180° C) for approximately 18 minutes, and take them out when a toothpick inserted in the center of each plum cake comes out clean. Store in the freezer for at least 8 hours before taking them out of the mold.

3 In a saucepan melt the fondant over low heat, add a little red food coloring, and stir until well blended. Take the plum cakes out of the mold and place them on a wire rack. Pour the fondant over them and spread it in a thin layer.

4 Using a hand mixer, whip the vegetable cream and mix with coloring and essential oil. Place it into a pastry bag and decorate each mini plum cake. Store them in the refrigerator for 1 hour until the whipped cream is completely chilled.

CHOCOLATE MINI PLUM CAKES
with Pistachio Cream and Cherry Jelly

Ingredients YIELDS 16

· 2 ⅓ cups (295 g) flour · ¼ cup (20 g) cacao · 1 cup (210 g) brown sugar · 1 ½ teaspoons baking powder · ½ teaspoon baking soda · ½ teaspoon salt · 1 teaspoon vanilla extract · 1.25 ounces (35 g) 70 percent chocolate · 6.5 ounces (200 g) soy milk · ⅓ cup (90 g) sunflower oil

Jelly:

· ¾ cup (200 g) cherry juice · ¼ cup (60 g) water · ⅓ cup (60 g) sugar · 1 teaspoon (2 g) agar

Decoration:

· 3 cups (720 g) creamy cheese (see recipe on p. 18) · 2 ½ tablespoons (40 g) pistachio paste · cherry jelly

1 In a bowl, mix all dry ingredients. Chop the chocolate and add soy milk, oil, and vanilla extract. Beat with a whisk until you get a smooth batter. Add the chocolate and continue beating for 1 minute. Use the batter to fill each cupcake liner halfway.

2 Bake at 355° F (180° C) for approximately 18 minutes, and take them out when a toothpick inserted in the center of each plum cake comes out clean. Store in the freezer for at least 8 hours before taking them out of the mold.

3 In a saucepan, mix the water, sugar, agar, and cherry juice. Place over heat and when it has started to boil, pour the mixture inside a rectangular mold. Chill it in the refrigerator.

4 Mix the creamy cheese and pistachio paste until its texture is completely smooth. Use this cream to decorate each mini plum cake. Cut the jelly into small pieces and use it to decorate each piece.

MINI CHOCOLATE PLUM CAKES
with Vanilla Cream and Black Olives

Ingredients YIELDS 16
· 2 ½ cups (315 g) flour · 1 cup (210 g) brown sugar · 2 teaspoons baking powder · ½ teaspoon salt · 1 teaspoon vanilla extract · 1.75 ounces (50 g) 50 percent chocolate · 6.5 ounces (200 g) soy milk · ⅓ cup (90 g) sunflower oil

Decoration:
· 3 cups (720 g) creamy cheese (see recipe on p. 18) · 2 vanilla beans · Kalamata olives

1 In a bowl, mix all dry ingredients (flour, sugar, salt, and baking powder). Chop the chocolate into small irregular pieces. Add the soy milk, oil, and vanilla extract to bowl. Mix using a whisk until you have a smooth and even batter. Add the chocolate and continue beating for 1 minute to mix it well with the batter. Use the batter to fill each mini plum cake liner halfway.

2 Bake at 355° F (180° C) for approximately 18 minutes, and take them out when a toothpick inserted in the center of each plum cake comes out clean. Store in the freezer for at least 8 hours before taking them out of the mold.

3 Cut the vanilla beans in half and scrape the seeds with a knife. Mix the creamy cheese and vanilla seeds. Decorate each mini plum cake with this mixture. De-pit a few olives and cut them into irregular pieces to decorate each piece.

Mini Plum Cakes
with PASSION FRUIT and Mango Jelly

Ingredients YIELDS 16
2 ½ cups (310 g) flour · 1 cup (220 g) brown sugar · 2 teaspoons baking powder · ½ teaspoon salt · ¼ teaspoon ground cardamom · ¼ teaspoon cinnamon · 1 teaspoon vanilla extract · ¾ cup (200 g) passion fruit juice · ½ cup (120 g) sunflower oil · sesame seeds

Jelly:
¾ cup (200 g) mango juice · ¼ cup (60 g) water · 2 ½ tablespoons (30 g) sugar · 1 teaspoon (2 g) agar

Decoration:
3 cups (720 g) margarine cream (see recipe on p. 21) · ½ teaspoon (2 g) passion fruit essential oil · yellow food coloring · mango jelly

1 In a bowl, mix all dry ingredients (flour, sugar, salt, cinnamon, cardamom, and baking powder).

Add passion fruit juice, oil, and vanilla extract to bowl. Mix with a whisk until you have a smooth and even batter. Use the batter to fill each mini plum cake liner and sprinkle with a pinch of sesame.

2 Bake at 355° F (180° C) for approximately 20 minutes, and take them out when a toothpick inserted in the center of each plum cake comes out clean. Store in the freezer for at least 8 hours before taking them out of the mold.

3 To make the jelly, in a saucepan mix the water, sugar, agar, and mango juice. Place it over medium heat and when it starts to boil, pour the mixture into a rectangular mold. Chill it in the refrigerator.

4 Mix the margarine cream, passion fruit essential oil, and food coloring. Decorate each mini plum cake with this mixture. Cut the jelly into small cubes and use them to decorate each piece.

Mini Lemon Plum Cakes
with HAZELNUT PRALINE and
Chocolate

Ingredients YIELDS 16
· 2 ½ cups (305 g) flour · 1 cup (210 g) brown sugar · 1 teaspoon baking soda · ½ teaspoon salt · 1 teaspoon vanilla extract · 1 cup (200 g) lemon juice · 1 lemon · ½ cup (120 g) sunflower oil · a dash of sesame seeds

Crunchy bits:
· 1.25 ounces (35 g) 50 percent chocolate · ¾ cup (75 g) wafers · 3 ounces (90 g) hazelnut praline

Decoration:
· 1 ⅓ cups (320 g) vegan cream cheese · 1 cup (240 g) vegetable whipping cream · 5.5 ounces (160 g) crunchy hazelnut praline and 50 percent chocolate · 1 teaspoon vanilla extract

1 In a bowl, mix all dry ingredients (flour, sugar, salt, and baking soda). Add lemon juice, oil, and vanilla extract. Using a wire whip, beat until you have a smooth, even batter. Grate the lemon peel and mix it with the lemon cake batter. Fill each mini plum cake liner with this dough and sprinkle a dash of sesame seeds on top.

2 Bake at 355° F (180° C) for approximately 20 minutes, and take them out when a toothpick inserted in the center of each plum cake comes out clean. Store in the freezer for at least 8 hours before taking them out of the mold.

3 To make the crunchy bits, melt the chocolate and mix it with hazelnut praline. Finely grind the wafers and mix them with chocolate praline.

4 Mix the cream cheese with 5.5 ounces (160 g) of crunchy praline. Whip the vegetable cream with vanilla extract and add it to the cream cheese mixture with praline. Beat well until you have a smooth cream. Take the mini plum cakes out of the mold and garnish them with crispy praline cream.

Madeleines with FLAVORED WHIPPED Cream

Ingredients YIELDS 8

· 2 cups (240 g) flour · 1 cup (200 g) brown sugar · 2 teaspoons baking powder · ½ teaspoon salt · ¼ teaspoon cinnamon · 1 lemon · 1 orange · 1 teaspoon vanilla extract · ⅓ cup (80 g) cornstarch · 6.5 ounces (200 g) soy milk · ⅓ cup (80 g) sunflower oil · 7 ½ tablespoons (100 g) olive oil · sugar

Decoration:
· ¾ cup (200 g) vegetable whipping cream · 3 tablespoons (35 g) sugar · ¼ cup (50 g) water · 1 orange · 1 lemon

1 In a bowl, mix all dry ingredients (flour, sugar, salt, cinnamon, and baking powder). Grate the lemon peel and orange peel. Dilute the cornstarch with soy milk. Add the mixture to the bowl of flour. Add the sunflower oil, olive oil, lemon peel, orange peel, and vanilla extract. Mix with a whisk until you have a smooth and even batter. Use the batter to fill each cupcake liner halfway and sprinkle a little sugar on top.

2 Bake at 355° F (180° C) for approximately 22 minutes, and take them out when a toothpick inserted in the center of each cupcake comes out clean. Store in a cool place for 3 hours.

3 In a saucepan, mix the cream, water, and sugar. Add the lemon peel and orange peel. Place it over medium heat and let boil for 2 minutes. Take out the peels using a sieve and store it in the refrigerator for at least 4 hours. Whip the flavored cream and decorate each madeleine.

PEAR CUPCAKES with
Chestnut Cream and Cognac

Ingredients YIELDS 12

· 1 ⅔ cups (200 g) flour · ¾ cup (165 g) brown sugar · 1 ½ teaspoons baking powder · ¼ teaspoon salt · ¼ teaspoon cinnamon · 1 orange · 1 teaspoon vanilla extract · ½ cup (65 g) cornstarch · ¾ cup (165 g) water · ⅓ cup (70 g) sunflower oil · 6 tablespoons (80 g) olive oil · 1 cup (200 g) pear (2 pieces) · cognac

Decoration:

· 1 ⅓ sticks (150 g) margarine · 1 ¾ (210 g) icing sugar · 2 tablespoons cognac · 1 cup (330 g) chestnut puree · marron glacé

1 In a bowl, mix all dry ingredients (flour, sugar, salt, cinnamon, and baking powder). Peel and dice the pears. Grate the orange peel. Dilute the cornstarch with water and add this mixture to the bowl of flour. Add the sunflower oil, olive oil, orange peel, and vanilla extract. Mix with a whisk until you have a smooth and even batter. Use the batter to fill each cupcake liner halfway.

2 Bake at 355° F (180° C) for approximately 24 minutes, and take them out when a toothpick inserted in the center of each cupcake comes out clean. Using a basting brush, top each cupcake with a little brandy and store them in the refrigerator for at least 3 hours.

3 To make the cream, mix margarine and powdered sugar using a whisk until you have a smooth cream with no lumps. In intervals, add the cognac and chestnut puree. Continue beating until you have a smooth and stable cream. Decorate each cupcake with chestnut cream and cognac. Serve each piece with marron glacé.

FIG and Raspberry Cupcakes

Ingredients YIELDS 12

· 2 ⅓ cups (300 g) flour · 1 cup (220 g) sugar · 1 teaspoon baking powder · ½ teaspoon baking soda · ½ teaspoon salt · 1 teaspoon vanilla extract · 6.4 ounces (190 g) soy milk · ½ cup (110 g) sunflower oil · 24 raspberries · 3 figs · Grand Marnier liqueur

Decoration:
· 3 cups (720 g) buttercream · ½ teaspoon raspberry essential oil · red food coloring · 3 figs

1 In a bowl, mix all dry ingredients (flour, sugar, baking soda, salt, and baking powder). Peel and cut the figs into quarters. Add the soy milk, oil, and vanilla extract to bowl. Mix with a whisk until you have a smooth and even batter. Use the batter to fill each cupcake liner halfway. Place on each cupcake two raspberries and one-quarter fig.

2 Bake at 355° F (180° C) for approximately 24 minutes, and take them out when a toothpick inserted in the center of each cupcake comes out clean. Store them in a cool place for a couple of hours. Using a basting brush, top each cupcake with a little Grand Marnier and store them in the refrigerator for at least 3 hours.

3 To make the decoration, mix buttercream, raspberry essential oil, and red food coloring to taste. Cut the figs into quarters. Decorate each cupcake with raspberry buttercream and one-quarter fig.

CRISPY
Lime and Hazelnut Cupcakes

Ingredients YIELDS 12
· 2 ⅓ cups (300 g) flour · 1 cup (220 g) sugar · 1 teaspoon baking powder · 1 teaspoon baking soda · ½ teaspoon salt · 1 teaspoon vanilla extract · 6.5 ounces (200 g) soy milk · ¾ cup (160 g) sunflower oil · ⅓ cup (40 g) raisins · 1.75 ounces (50 g) chopped 53 percent chocolate · 1 lime

Cream:
· 2 cups (500 g) vegetable whipping cream · 10 ounces (300 g) 53 percent chocolate · ½ stick (65 g) margarine

Crunchy bits:
· ⅓ stick (40 g) margarine · 3.5 ounces (100 g) 53 percent chocolate · 13 ounces (380 g) hazelnut praline · 1 ⅔ cups (190 g) neulas or crushed cookies

1 In a bowl, mix all dry ingredients. Add the soy milk, oil, and vanilla. Beat with a whisk. In another bowl, mix the raisins, grated lime peel, and chocolate. Combine both mixtures and continue to beat.

Use the batter to fill each cupcake liner halfway. Bake at 355° F (180° C) for approximately 27 minutes, and Store in a cool place for 2 hours.

2 To make the cream, boil the cream and pour it over the chocolate and margarine. Emulsify with a hand mixer until you have a smooth cream with no lumps. Store in the refrigerator for 6 to 12 hours.

3 To make the crunchy bits, melt margarine and chocolate in a bowl. Add the praline and cookies or neulas. Mix half of the batter and place it in a 3x3-inch (8x8 cm) frame. Store in the refrigerator for 1 hour and then cut into sixty cubes.

4 Cover the top of each cupcake with the remaining batter and place in the refrigerator for 1 hour. Decorate each cupcake with the chocolate cream and five crunchy hazelnut dice.

CHOCOLATE and
Whipped Cream Cupcakes

Ingredients YIELDS 12
· 1 ½ cups (190 g) flour · ¾ cup (70 g) cacao · 1 cup (220 g) sugar · 2 teaspoons baking powder · ½ teaspoon salt · 1 teaspoon vanilla extract · ⅓ cup (50 g) cornstarch · 6.75 ounces (200 g) water · 2.8 ounces (80 g) 70 percent chocolate · 1 ¼ sticks (145 g) margarine

Filling:
· vegan cacao cream

Decoration:
· 1 ½ cups (375 g) vegetable cream · ¼ cup (55 g) sugar · 2.8 ounces (80 g) 70 percent chocolate · 70 percent chocolate shortbread (see recipe on p. 29)

1 In a bowl, mix all dry ingredients (flour, sugar, cacao, salt, and baking powder). In another bowl, mix the water and cornstarch. And in a third bowl, melt the margarine and chocolate. To the bowl with dry ingredients, add these other two mixtures and the vanilla. Mix until you have a smooth batter. Use the batter to fill each cupcake liner halfway. Bake at 355° F (180° C) for approximately 24 minutes, and store in a cool place for a couple of hours.

2 To make the filling, melt the cacao cream in a microwave or a double boiler. Place it in a pastry bag with a nozzle. Prick each cupcake with the pastry bag and fill it with whipped cream.

3 To make the decoration, place the vegetable cream and sugar on low heat until it starts boiling. Pour the mixture into a bowl and add the chocolate. Mix until you have a smooth cream with no lumps, and then store it in the refrigerator for 4 hours. Decorate each cupcake with whipped cream and chocolate shortbread.

ANISE, CARAMEL, and
Chocolate Cupcakes

Ingredients YIELDS 12

· 1 ⅓ cups (200 g) wheat flour · ½ cup
(55 g) almond flour · ⅔ cup (60 g) cacao ·
1 cup (220 g) sugar · 2 teaspoons baking
powder · ½ teaspoon salt · 1 teaspoon
vanilla extract · 6 ounces (175 g) almond
milk · 2.8 ounces (80 g) 70 percent
chocolate · ½ cup (120 g) sunflower oil

Cream:
· 3 cups (660 g) creamy cheese (see recipe
on p. 18) · ⅔ cup (85 g) toffee (see recipe
on p. 20) · 3 tablespoons (45 ml) anise

Flakes:
· 3.5 ounces (100 g) 70 percent chocolate
· 1 sheet of parchment paper or PVC

Decoration:
· anise and caramel cream · toffee
· 70 percent chocolate flakes

1 In a bowl, mix the dry ingredients. In another
bowl, melt the chocolate and oil. Add almond milk,
chocolate, oil, and vanilla to the bowl of flour. Beat well
and use this batter to fill each cupcake liner halfway.
Bake at 355° F (180° C) for approximately 22 minutes,
and store in a cool place for 2 hours.

2 To make the cream, beat anise and toffee in a bowl,
and add them to the creamy cheese. Mix using
a spatula in a rolling motion so that the bubble goes
down as much as possible. Decorate each cupcake with
cream and store them in the refrigerator for at least 4
hours.

3 To make the flakes, melt the chocolate at 120° F (50°
C) until smooth, and let it cool down to 90° F (32° C).
Pour it on a piece of parchment paper and spread it with
a spatula until the layer is very thin. Cut 1x1-inch (3x3
cm) squares and place a weight on top so they do not
warp when they crystallize.

4 To finish making the decoration, place the toffee
in a pastry bag with a nozzle and squeeze it into
each of the cupcakes. Finally, place a chocolate square
on top.

COOKIES,
Cream, and Shortbread Cupcakes

Ingredients YIELDS 12
· 1 ¾ cups (230 g) flour · ¾ cup (70 g) cacao · 1 cup (220 g) sugar · 1 teaspoon baking powder · 1 teaspoon baking soda · ½ teaspoon salt · 2 teaspoons vanilla extract · 6.5 ounces (200 g) soy milk · ¾ cup (160 g) sunflower oil · ½ cup (60 g) chocolate shortbread (see recipe on p. 29)

Cream:
· 3 cups (720 g) margarine cream · 1 teaspoon vanilla extract · ¾ cup (85 g) chocolate shortbread

Decoration:
· Margarine, vanilla, and shortbread cream · 12 chocolate shortbread pieces

1. In a bowl, mix all dry ingredients (flour, cacao, sugar, baking soda, salt, and baking powder). Chop chocolate shortbread into little pieces. Add the soy milk, oil, and vanilla extract. Whip using a wire whisk. Add the shortbread and continue beating until you get a smooth batter. Use the batter to fill each cupcake liner halfway.

2. Bake at 355° F (180° C) for approximately 24 minutes, and take them out when a toothpick inserted in the center of each cupcake comes out clean. Store them in a cool place for a couple of hours.

3. To make the cream, chop or grind the shortbread and add the margarine cream and vanilla extract. Mix until you get a smooth cream.

4. Decorate each cupcake with cream and chocolate shortbread on top.

CHOCOLATE and Peanut Cupcakes

Ingredients YIELDS 12

· 1 ¾ cups (230 g) flour · ¾ cup (70 g) cacao · 1 cup (220 g) sugar · 1 teaspoon baking powder · 1 teaspoon baking soda · ½ teaspoon salt · 2 teaspoons vanilla extract · 6.5 ounces (200 g) soy milk · ¾ cup (160 g) sunflower oil · ⅓ cup (50 g) salted peanuts

Cream:

· 1 ¾ cups (420 g) vegetable whipping cream · ¼ stick (30 g) margarine · ⅓ cup (100 g) peanut butter

Decoration:

· peanut butter · sparkling chocolate icing (see recipe on p. 26) · vegan cacao cream

1 In a bowl, mix all dry ingredients (flour, cacao, sugar, baking soda, salt, and baking powder). Chop salted peanuts. Add the soy milk, oil, and vanilla extract. Whip using a wire whisk. Add the chopped peanuts and continue beating until you get a smooth batter. Use the batter to fill each cupcake liner halfway. Bake at 355° F (180° C) for approximately 25 minutes, and take them out when a toothpick inserted in the center of each cupcake comes out clean. Store them in a cool place for a couple of hours.

2 To make the cream, melt the margarine and peanut butter in a microwave or double boiler and beat well. Whip the vegetable cream, add it to the mixture, and mix with a spatula.

3 Place the cream in a pastry bag with a round tip and decorate each cupcake. Store the decorated cupcake in the freezer. Melt the glaze and spread it on top of each cupcake. Melt the chocolate cream and pour it into a pastry bag with a fine nozzle and decorate each cupcake. Thaw cupcakes for 2 hours in the refrigerator before serving.

GIN and Passion Fruit Cupcakes

Ingredients YIELDS 12
· 2 ½ cups (300 g) flour · 1 cup (220 g) sugar · 2 teaspoons baking powder · ½ teaspoon baking soda · ½ teaspoon salt · ¾ cup (200 g) passion fruit juice · 1 teaspoon vanilla extract · ⅔ cup (130 g) sunflower oil · 1 lemon

Cream:
· 10 cups (600 g) white chocolate whipped cream · 3 tablespoons (45 g) Seagram's gin

Decoration:
· white chocolate cream and gin
· 3 pieces of passion fruit

1. In a bowl, mix all dry ingredients (flour, sugar, baking soda, salt, and baking powder). Add the passion fruit juice, vanilla extract, grated lemon peel, and oil. Whip using a wire whisk.

Use the batter to fill each cupcake liner halfway.

2. Bake at 355° F (180° C) for approximately 24 minutes, and take them out when a toothpick inserted in the center of each cupcake comes out clean. Store them in a cool place for a couple of hours.

3. To make the cream, whip the whipping cream, add the gin, and stir with a spatula, making circular motions so that the cream does not lose its bubbles.

4. Decorate cupcakes with cream and passion fruit pulp.

Alphabetized recipes